SWANS

SWANS

Teiji Saga

Introduction by Janet Kear

RIZZOLI
NEW YORK

First published in the United States of America in 1990 by
Rizzoli International Publications, Inc.
300 Park Avenue South, New York, New York 10010

Copyright © 1990 by Teiji Saga and Schirmer/Mosel, Munich

Library of Congress Cataloging-in-Publication Data

Saga, Teiji, 1919-
    [Schwäne. English]
    Swans : photographs / by Teiji Saga ; introduction by Janet Kear.
        p.   cm.
    First published with the German title: Schwäne, but with an
English introduction.
    ISBN 0-8478-1293-6
    1. Whooper swan. 2. Whooper swan — Japan — Hokkaido — Pictorial
works. I. Kear, Janet. II. Title.
QL696.A52S2413 1990
598.4′1 — dc20   90-53157
                                                  CIP

Design layout by Mary McBride
Color separations by O.R.T. Kirchner & Graser, Berlin
Printed by Appl, Wemding
Bound by Hollmann, Darmstadt
Printed in West Germany
A Schirmer/Mosel Production

The Whooper Swan

Strikingly elegant, with long neck and noble-looking head, white plumage, a yellow-and-black bill, and black legs, the Whooper swan is one of the largest birds of Europe and Asia. Its scientific name *Cygnus cygnus* was devised by the great Swedish taxonomist Linnaeus in the middle of the eighteenth century and honors Cygnus, beautiful son of the Greek god Apollo, who was transformed into a swan after leaping to his death in a lake. On the other hand, the bird's common name in many European languages refers to its loud and melodious voice: Whooper in English, *Singschwan* in German, *Sangsvan* in Swedish, and *Cisne cantor* in Spanish. The false legend of the "swan song" — that swans sing before they die — was known to Plato, to Aristotle who wrote that they "are musical, and sing chiefly at the approach of death," and to Shakespeare who refers to the tradition in *Othello*. The idea may have originated in an uncomprehending observation of migration; in spring, swans went away to lands unknown and, before departure, were particularly restless, flying around and calling in order to encourage the family and flock to be up and gone. Perhaps early man associated the swans' song overhead with the birds' disappearance, and their "music" with imminent death.

There are eight types of swans in the world which all belong to the wildfowl group of ducks, geese, and swans. Their nearest relatives are the grazing geese with whom they share a number of behavioral features including a well-developed family life and a firm pair-bond between male and female. Swans and geese are therefore classified together in the same tribe; both are perhaps more primitive than ducks and considerably larger. In the course of evolution, swans appeared first, and a line from them eventually gave rise to the goose. Whereas geese are confined to the grasslands of the northern hemisphere, swans are more widespread and found in many lowland fresh waters, being rare only in the tropics and absent entirely from equatorial and southern Africa.

Differences between swans and geese are mostly matters of degree—a relatively larger foot or longer neck—but all swans are larger than geese, and, except for the peculiar Coscoroba swan of South America, the adult birds have bare, unfeathered skin between the eyes and the bill. They incubate their eggs longer (the Black swan of Australia for thirty-nine days), take longer to mature to the flying stage, and never breed until they are at least three years old, although geese can lay when they are only two. The male swan helps build the nest, something the male goose never does. Swans also provide food for their newly-hatched young by plucking underwater or overhead vegetation, and by foot-paddling to raise edible items to the surface. They fly, as do geese, in diagonal lines or V-shaped formations.

Of the eight swans (Mute, Black, Black-necked, Coscoroba, Trumpeter, Whooper, Whistling, and Bewick's), the last four are clearly more closely related than the rest. These are the so-called "northern swans" of Europe, Asia, and North America; all are white when adult and have black or yellow-and-black bills with no bill-knobs. They are migratory, highly territorial when nesting yet gregarious in winter, and have loud voices. The Whooper swan's closest cousin is probably the rarest of all—the Trumpeter of North America, which is larger and has a similarly flat profile to its head. The Whooper, Bewick's, and semi-domesticated Mute swan of Eurasia sometimes winter together and may be difficult to tell apart at a distance; indeed, the Bewick's swan was only generally recognized to be different from the Whooper after a description published in the Journal of the Linnaen Society, written by London businessman William Yarrell in 1830.

Description.

The Whooper swan is one of our largest flying birds; the average female weighs eighteen pounds and the average male twenty-one pounds, although one Danish bird scaled over thirty pounds. Males are thus about thirteen percent heavier than females. Their "whooping" voice is due to a long and convoluted windpipe that grows into the breastbone as the bird matures and, in the adult of both sexes, produces a far-reaching, resonating sound, lower in pitch than that of the Bewick's. Whoopers use their voices in circumstances that keep the family and flock together, in preflight signals with head-bobbing to integrate the flying of the group, and in the triumph ceremony performed between members of a mated pair after they have driven off an enemy. During their first winter, cygnets have squeaky voices, gray-brown plumage, and bills that are grayish with a touch of pink; they are noticeably smaller than their parents and have characteristically shorter wings. As the season progresses, they acquire white feathering, and their bills turn first white, then pale yellow, and finally the bright chrome-yellow-and-black of adulthood. Young Whoopers rarely retain traces of gray juvenile plumage after their first year, unlike the young of Bewick's and Mute swans. The iris of the adult's eye is brown or occasionally blue-gray. Russet-stained heads and necks, from the ferrous salts of the water in which they feed, are a noticeable feature of Whoopers from Iceland.

A longer neck in proportion to its body distinguishes the Whooper from the smaller Bewick's; the Whooper also has a flatter forehead and a longer bill in proportion to its total head length. The amount of yellow at the base of the bill varies from one individual to another, but much less so than in the Bewick's swan. The patch always makes an acute angle at the lower edge of the upper mandible, extending beyond the nostril, whereas in the Bewick's it ends bluntly above the nostril. Adult Mute swans have orange bills with black tips and pronounced black knobs on their foreheads; they hold their necks in a more graceful curve than the other two swans, and raise their wing feathers above their backs when they are angry.

Range and population size.
A marked retraction in the breeding range of the western population of Whooper swans was apparent until relatively recently; now protection has resulted in the establishment of new nesting sites in a number of countries including Iceland, Sweden, and Finland. Major declines also occurred during the nineteenth century in the Soviet Union due to hunting and disturbance of nesting areas, and a slight fall is still being recorded there.

The world population of Whoopers is estimated to be around 100,000. The breeding range is south of that of the Bewick's swan and extends from Iceland across northern Russia to the Urals and on through the reed-fringed lakes of the Siberian steppes, sometimes into the "taigu" forest of the boreal region, to the Pacific coast. Each sub-population has a different migratory flyway and winter destination. Britain and Ireland have about 15,400 Whoopers in winter, most of which are thought to originate from Iceland. This figure was reached as the result of a weekend census in January 1986, using a large volunteer workforce that regularly went out and counted the birds.

The Whooper once bred in the Orkney Islands off northern Scotland, perhaps regularly until the eighteenth century; now the few nesting attempts in Britain seem to be by injured birds unable to make the long journey to Iceland. However, not all Iceland's breeding swans migrate; some 1,300 remain in brackish or warm thermal waters in the south, and a few have taken to gathering in winter on the lake in Reykjavík where the water is kept open and they are fed. They only move overseas if the weather is particularly bad and the natural and unnatural food supplies run out. Ringing (securing a ring around the bird's neck for identification purposes) suggests that the vast majority of Whooper swans leaving Iceland come to the British Isles, mainly Ireland and Scotland, but a few have been seen in winter in Norway, Denmark, and the Netherlands.

There are two other sub-populations in the western Palearctic region besides the Icelandic one. The 25,000 Whoopers of northwest Europe breed in the region of Finno-Scandia and western Siberia and pass through the Baltic states to winter in southern Norway and Sweden, Denmark, and the Schleswig-Holstein and Mecklenburg districts of Germany. The third group of 17,000 birds nests in central Siberia and winters on the Black and Caspian seas, with a few hundred traveling into Greece. There are other breeding swans in eastern Siberia, Outer Mongolia, and Sakhalin, that winter in Korea (2–3,000), China, and Japan. Figures for China are hard to obtain, but over 10,000 winter in Japan, where they appear mainly in Hokkaido and northern Honshu, and are particularly common at Kominato Bay and Hyoko, both of which, because of the swans, have been declared natural monuments.

The Whooper swan also winters in the outer Aleutians and Commander Islands, and is occasionally reported in Wrangell Island and Greenland. It is replaced ecologically by the Trumpeter swan across Alaska, Canada, and the United States, just as the Eurasian Bewick's swan is replaced in the tundra of North America by its close relative, the slightly larger Whistling swan.

Tradition is an important aspect of the lives of swans; they tend to follow the same routes, to the same territory, and to familiar wintering sites. Thus individuals add to their own accumulated experience and to that of previous generations; the cygnets stay with their parents for ten months to learn migration paths, safe field and wetland systems in which to feed and roost, and, equally necessary, places to avoid.

The swans' year.
If a male and female are to breed, they must defend a reedy, shallow, lakeland territory of perhaps 250 acres, approximately two miles from the nest of their nearest neighbors. The Whooper swan takes one hundred and thirty days to complete its breeding cycle so that the territory, on which most pairs will remain in isolation until the young can fly, must be ice-free for that period if a successful season is to result. In Finland, some families are mobile after the cygnets hatch, but they seem to pay a penalty in that they produce smaller clutches and raise fewer offspring. What determines when the pair will start to breed? The most significant environmental feature that regulates the time when birds put on fat, migrate, display, lay eggs, and molt is daylight, or the pattern of increasing and decreasing length of day. Other, less regular climatic changes that may affect the exact date of egg laying are temperature, days of frost and snow, rainfall, hours of sunshine, and wind speeds.

Visual and auditory displays are the means of indicating to other swans that a bird is threatening, submissive, or in courting mood. Head-bobbing is the normal greeting, and courtship is likewise relatively inconspicuous. It is seen in the juvenile flocks during pair formation when the male and female face one another on the water, breast to breast, with their chins tucked in and bill tips crossed. The triumph ceremony consists of waving the wings in a half-opened and lifted position while the neck is repeatedly bent and extended as the two birds, or occasionally the whole family, call. When either one of the pair calls, the other normally joins in. Displays at copulation, which may occur in winter, on the journey north, or on the breeding ground, start with synchronized head-dipping movements that closely resemble bathing. The male mounts for only a few moments, holding on to the feathers of the female's neck, and, afterwards, both birds rise in the water, calling softly before settling back to preening, washing, and tail-wagging.

Aggression towards a flying intruder is communicated by a warning display of half-opened, quivering wings and a great deal of loud calling. A swan on the water will indicate threat by pointing its bill straight forward and ruffling the feathers of its neck. One that is not about to fight will have its neck plumage sleaked and its head pointing down.

As in all northern swans, the conspicuous white plumage of the two adults and their voices play an important part in advertizing their ownership of a territory, thus keeping others away. Nests are built of marsh materials; typically they are about forty inches across and twenty inches high, and always close to water. Often the nest of the previous year will be used again if young hatched there. In Finland, visits to the site start even before the mound is free of snow. Building is done by both members of the pair, but mostly by the female. The large cream-colored eggs weigh eleven ounces on average and are laid at two day intervals at the end of April, if the weather is warm, and during early May in cold years when the ice melts slowly. In Finland, May 25th seems to be the critical date by which egg laying must start if the brood is to fledge before the snow returns. In some years, pairs may not breed at all. The clutch size will depend partly on how early in the season eggs are laid, but is on average smaller in Iceland than in Continental Europe, four as opposed to five eggs being normal; the maximum number of eggs anywhere is seven or, very rarely, eight.

Incubation, which starts with the laying of the last egg, will continue for about thirty-one days and is performed entirely by the female. She uses her chin and bill to turn the eggs just under once an hour, mostly along their long axis, and twice a day she will leave the nest to feed and drink while her mate stands guard. Hatching starts with the last egg to be laid and takes over thirty-six hours from the moment that sounds are heard within the shells.

The large gray cygnets weigh about eight ounces at a day old, and more than twenty-five percent of their body consists of a yolk sac. This yolk is drawn into the abdomen during the hatching process and is rich in fats and protein that will provide nourishment during the first week of life. The youngsters are delightful, with pink bills and legs and gruff voices. Like all wildfowl, they do not hatch with an instinctive knowledge of their own kind but learn to accept as parents the first moving things that they see—usually, of course, their mother and father. On the second morning, they are led to the water and start feeding, but their mother will brood them beneath her wings when they are tired, cold, or wet, often returning with them to the nest. The cygnet's husky voice is important in indicating that it is lost, cold, sleepy, hurt, threatened, or content, and in eliciting the appropriate response. Communication with its mother and with brothers and sisters in the brood starts while the young bird is still in the egg. First clicks are heard, then cheeps; the mother responds by calling softly, and presumably both parent and cygnet become familiar with one another's calls.

At first, the young eat insects on or near the water surface, as well as the soft parts of plants. Some food items are found for them by the raking and paddling movements of their parents' feet. The proportion of vegetable matter in the diet will increase as they develop, and, with high protein food and twenty-four hours of daylight, growth and feathering are rapid. At about eighty days, the wings are long enough for the birds to take their first flight. There is still feathering between the eyes and the bill, but this is gradually rubbed off. White feathers begin to replace the gray ones almost as soon as the swan is fully grown (except for the wing and tail quills, which will not be molted until the following summer). Ultimately, the male will be on average thirteen percent larger than the female, but the sex of an adult in the field can only be guessed at, since the overlap in size is considerable. While the cygnets are small, the adults lose and then regrow their wing feathers at a rate of about a quarter of an inch a day, and are unable to fly for over a month (first the female, then the male, so that one parent is always able to defend the family).

Pre-breeding juveniles, or those adults who lose their eggs early and give up the energetic business of defending a territory, may go on a molt migration to a remote traditional wetland with a good food supply and minimal disturbance; here they will pass their flightless period in company with others, and in relative calm and safety.

Migration southwards starts as days shorten in September or early October, and Icelandic birds tend to leave in north-westerly airstreams. Do they use the stars, moon, and sun to keep themselves on course? We do not know; however, we are certain that they fly high, where strong jet winds can help them on their way. A party of Whoopers was observed from an aircraft over the Inner Hebrides in December 1967, flying south at an altitude of 25,000 feet. The swans were in northerly winds and were assumed to have originated from Iceland in a ridge of high pressure at dawn. Calculations showed that they would reach their destination in Ireland after only seven hours and that they were flying at the incredibly low temperature of $-54°F$. Flights at such high levels allow faster journeys, and, surprisingly, altitude does not pose breathing problems since the blood circulation of birds is very efficient, and low temperatures in clear air have little adverse effect. In clouds, supercooling might result in the icing of the plumage. Journeys overland by birds breeding and wintering in Continental Europe and Asia need not be so high, and the flocks can land to feed and rest. Their autumn flights tend to be more direct and rapid than spring flights; the birds appear on the steppes just ahead of the arrival of snow—thus the Russian saying that swans "carry the winter on their wings," suggesting a brief visit before hard weather closes in behind them.

The family tends to stay together until the spring, the male in particular continuing to defend his offspring so that they can spend most of their time feeding and putting on weight. In contrast to the Bewick's swan, however, the Whooper seems more loosely attached to its mate in winter—an extended family has more significance. The group is sometimes joined on migration or during the winter by the young of previous years and their newly acquired mates, and this large family can become quite dominant and aggressive within the flock. Dominance seems to be associated mainly with feeding rights, and disputes can be noisy. In the autumn at Martin Mere, when new Whoopers are arriving daily, one hears many loud arguments and sees the occasional spectacular battle. As winter progresses, a peck order is established and quarrels become less common. Fights can last for several minutes and involve the adult birds beating their opponents with the "wrists" of their wings and biting their shoulders, while cygnets and other group members shout abuse. Injury is almost never caused because one party gives in and swims away in submissive posture. In general, families that arrive early in the season and have a large number of members win more of their battles and are at the top of the hierarchy.

Spring flights pose more of a problem than autumn flights for Whooper swans that must return to Iceland, since, with most of the weather coming from the west, they are unable to predict conditions over the route and at their destination. Return movements start in anticyclonic conditions in mid-March and may go on until early May. Two waves of migration are seen into Finland; the breeders move early and fast (about one hundred miles a day), while the nonbreeders arrive in the nesting region a month later. The break up of the family occurs just before the adult pair reaches their breeding territory. The fact that clutch size in Iceland is smaller on average than it is elsewhere may be due to the higher energy requirements of birds that must make long overseas journeys, with no possibility of landing to feed, just before laying.

Sexual maturity is attained at three years, and pair formation may occur slowly one year earlier; however, successful breeding is delayed until a good territory can be found and perhaps fought for, and a few pairs may build a nest the summer before they lay for the first time. Flocks of immature, pre-breeding swans gather in large numbers in coastal bays or on large lakes in summer, feeding, sleeping, and getting to know a mate. Once made, the choice of partner is for life; divorce after the pair-bond is established is rare, especially if the birds have reared young (although one breeding pair of Whooper swans has been seen to separate since the Caerlaverock study started in 1980). If a partner dies, then most birds will re-mate within one season. Breeding is a costly business, and individuals who produce many cygnets every year do not live for long, while others who breed less vigorously attain a ripe old age.

Food and feeding.

The adult Whooper swan is almost entirely vegetarian, feeding (by reaching and upending with its long neck, and by raking with its powerful feet) on the roots, stems, leaves, and seeds of marshland plants such as waterstarwort *(Callitriche)*, water forget-me-not *(Myosotis scorpioides)*, water crowfoot *(Ranunculus), Chara,* and bur reed *(Sparganium emersum)*. The Whooper also grazes flooded pastures, walking quite well on land, with much less of a waddle than the Mute swan. *Lolium* and *Phleum* grasses are particularly favored, as are clover stolons *(Trifolium repens)*. This food is grasped by the bill and tongue, and large pieces are swallowed whole. In order to grind it down in its gizzard prior to digestion (no bird has teeth), the swan eats grit in the form of small stones and sand. Feeding at the coast on eelgrass or *Zostera,* which is done extensively, results in the enlargement of glands that are situated beneath the skin above the eyes and which are able to extract excess salt from the birds' blood. This allows them to eat vegetation from brackish water. These "nasal glands," inherited from reptilean ancestors, will function in any bird that occasionally drinks sea water. They have been lost in mammals who must rely on their relatively less efficient kidneys to rid themselves of unwanted salts in their food. In particular, Whoopers feed at sea in severe weather when inland lakes freeze and huge numbers congregate in sheltered inlets until conditions improve.

Since a succession of hard winters in the 1940s that made natural foods scarce, increasing numbers of birds in some parts of Britain and elsewhere are resorting to farmland such as grain stubbles. Winter wheat commonly follows potatoes in the Scottish farming rotation, and decaying waste potatoes are often found lying on the surface of the fields. These tubers were probably eaten sporadically by the swans for some years, but only during and after a series of severe winters did Whooper swans fly into harvested fields before any wheat had sprouted, purely to eat potatoes. Here they do no harm, but there are sometimes allegations of damage to grassland and clover in the spring, when the birds may be in competition with the farmer's sheep for the best pasture and graze, trample, and pull up green winter cereals. In Iceland, there are problems for agricultural interests when the large molting flocks of immature and nonbreeding swans feed on cultivated grassland all summer. A safe roost on lake or river, where the birds can spend the night surrounded by water, seems to be essential for the establishment of any new feeding ground. Within the breeding territories, mare's tail *(Hippuris vulgaris)* is the most important natural food, and an excellent supply may mean a large brood.

Artificial feeding by man has gradually become more common during the last four decades. Changes in winter distribution have occurred as a consequence. As well as bread in Reykjavík, Whooper swans are given grain and potatoes at Wildfowl and Wetlands Trust refuges at Welney, Martin Mere, and Caerlaverock in England and Scotland, grain at Kilcolman in Ireland, and rice, oats, corn, soya beans, bread, tea grounds, and greens at about fifteen sites, including the twenty-acre Lake Hyoko in Japan. All these places were selected by the birds as roosts before artificial feeding started, and the food is given to them at the edge of the water, so that they are never far from safety. They would, in other circumstances, be fearful of man, and their confidence in the person with the feed bucket is acquired over a few months during which they are protected from any other disturbance. Swans are gregarious in winter and traditionally return to the same place in autumn if conditions there were good in the past. Adult pairs will bring their cygnets, and so the flocks accumulate.

The Whoopers arrived first at Hyoko, a lake at the edge of the town of Suibara in Niigata Prefecture, in January 1950, when a fanatical conservationist and farmer called Jusaburo Koshikawa tamed about thirty of them by providing food. His vigorous protection meant that, within ten years, swan numbers had risen to four hundred and that they had been joined by many ducks who also enjoyed the safety and liberal meals of rice. In 1967, nearly seven hundred swans were counted, and by 1970 over a thousand were spending most of the winter on the lake where Shigeo Koshikawa continues his father's tradition of care. Many of the superb photographs in this book were taken at such sanctuaries in Japan.

Death.

Adult swans have few natural enemies except man, and Whoopers are no longer hunted in any part of their range. Instead, they tend to be cared for in harsh weather, so that mortality, at about twelve percent per year for adults, is relatively low in comparison with most ducks and geese. Nevertheless, eighty percent of those hatched will not reach breeding age, and many will die as cygnets from starvation and cold. The losses during the second week of life are probably highest, because by then the young birds have used up the reserves of yolk which sustain them through the first few days. In subsequent weeks, death is principally due to adverse weather, but predation also plays a part. In Iceland, where four eggs is the usual clutch, three cygnets is the normal brood, and the hazards of migration take a further toll of the young birds, so that brood size in Britain is 2.66 on average. X-rays of the bodies of one hundred Whoopers caught at Caerlaverock in 1989 showed that ten had lead pellets in their tissues. For a bird that is protected in Britain, Ireland, and Iceland, this is an unhappy state of affairs. Some of the pellets are perhaps coming from the guns of people deliberately firing at a protected animal, but most are there presumably because the bird was mistaken in dim light for a legitimate quarry goose. It is not known whether the lead in the muscles does the birds any lasting harm once initial wounds are healed, but it seems unlikely that it does them any good.

Lead poisoning can occur after the ingestion of shotgun pellets. Mistaken for grit, they are ground in the bird's gizzard into a lethal solution, causing the death of some swans on the wintering grounds. Powerlines, too, can be lethal. Sadly, collision with wires has become the commonest cause of death among Whooper swans in Britain — the haunting moan of the wind in the wires might be said to be their "swan song." The birds fly fast, and their eyesight is such that they cannot easily detect the thin cables ahead of them, especially at night and in fog; marking the lines conspicuously does help but cannot eliminate the problem completely. As a greater proportion of wintering flocks gather on reserves because of the provision of food and protection from disturbance, more swans will become susceptible to collision with the local cables. The fed swans may also be affected by the spread of disease, though this is unlikely if the roost and land around it are relatively birdfree in the summer when the sun's naturally disinfecting ultraviolet rays can get to work.

Cold weather is not necessarily harmful if it does not last too long. During snow storms, swans may sit on shore for a while with their feet tucked into their side feathers, facing the wind, with their bills, up to the nostrils, tucked beneath the plumage of their backs. Birds have no sweat glands and lose heat only from bare skin or from their lungs, so that this posture reduces heat loss to a minimum and allows the air breathed in to be warmed by the feathers. In the 1930s, the number of feathers on a Whistling swan was determined to be 25, 216, of which 20,177 are on the head and neck; together they account for ten percent of the total body weight. They provide excellent insulation but need constant attention to keep them in good order. Oil pollution can destroy their waterproofing qualities, and oiled swans may die of cold and from the toxic effects of the chemicals that they swallow as they attempt to preen.

Pesticides have also taken their toll. In the late 1960s, nearly forty Whoopers, a third of the local population, were found dead at one site in central Scotland. Their bodies contained traces of mercury picked up, it was thought, from newly sown winter wheat grains that had been treated with an agricultural dressing to destroy insect pests. Similar incidents of large-scale poisoning have occurred on Scottish farmland during the 1970s and 1980s.

A few lucky Whooper swans reach sixteen years of age in the wild. In captivity, they may live much longer — up to twenty-five or thirty years.

Ringing and research.

Much of the information gathered about swans—reproduction, mortality, distance traveled in a lifetime—is obtained only if an individual swan is recognizable and carries a ring on its leg. Until the mid-1960s, the ring was a narrow metal one made of a light alloy and stamped with a serial number and the address of the organization (usually a museum) to which the finder of the swan might write. Most such recoveries depended on the finding of a dead body. The invention at The Wildfowl Trust at Slimbridge, England, of large plastic rings, two inches wide, with numbers or letters three-fourths of an inch high that can be read up to nine hundred feet away using telescopes, has changed the situation drastically. Now the fortunes of single birds can be followed, and there is no need for repeated catches to examine a ring.

For instance in 1988, 365 Whoopers were ringed in Iceland by Wildfowl Trust and University of Iceland research staff; 105 birds were sighted during the following winter, 104 in the British Isles and one at Nissum Fjord, Denmark. An additional thirty-seven were ringed in Britain during the winter of 1988–1989, mostly at Caerlaverock in Scotland. Of nine ringed Whoopers on the Hundred Foot Washes near Welney in 1988–1989, five were seen to have been caught elsewhere, one at Caerlaverock and four in Iceland. During the summer of 1989, a further 185, including 47 cygnets, were marked in Iceland with yellow plastic legrings (and the tail feathers of 43 were dyed with a harmless yellow picric acid). Also caught were one swan previously banded at Caerlaverock and 28 ringed during the 1988 summer expedition. The yellow dye remains conspicuous for only six months, since the colored feathers are molted out during the following summer; its presence draws attention for a while to the fact that the bird is ringed and that the number on the ring can be read. The faithfulness of birds to their traditional wintering grounds has been well established—nearly eighty percent of Whoopers ringed at Caerlaverock returned for at least one more season.

Research into Whistling swans in North America in the early 1970s relied not on legrings, but on marking with plastic neckcollars, also engraved with numbers, and the birds are not thought to have come to any harm. Similar collars, about three inches high with an inside diameter of two inches, which are more visible to observers than legrings, have now been put on Whoopers in Iceland, Denmark, and Japan, and have produced additional insight into their movements. Collars, because they are so visible, can give far more information than metal or even plastic legrings. For instance, of the 116 Whoopers neckcollared in Denmark, more than twenty percent were seen abroad compared with only nine percent recoveries of 266 merely ringed; however, the collars do not last as long—in the Icelandic study using collars, although sixty-nine percent were resighted in the first year, all neckbands had disappeared within three years. Radio transmitters can produce even more data in the short term but are, at the moment, expensive and difficult to handle satisfactorily. However, a bird with an operating transmitter has flown recently from Iceland to Colonsay in Scotland.

In order to be ringed, birds must be caught. This can be done with a shepherd's crook hooked around the neck during the summer while the adults are molting and before the young can fly, or in the winter in "swan pipes." The first "swan pipe" — a ditch covered by netting at the corner of the lake on which the birds were fed — was built in 1969 to catch Bewick's swans at Slimbridge. The swans are enticed by grain spread along the water's edge under the nets of the "pipe." When sufficient numbers are beneath the netting, someone appears between them and the lake, apparently cutting off any means of escape, and they are walked into a cage trap at the other end of the device. Once caught, the birds are quite docile. They are given two rings: the standard metal one, which usually remains on them for life, and a large, lettered plastic one on the other leg. The plastic is not as tough as metal and may be shattered and lost if it is hit hard, especially in cold weather. A totally indestructible large ring might damage the bird itself, and that would be unacceptable to the researchers. While the swan is being ringed and sexed by cloacal examination (the plastic ring is placed on the right leg of males and the left of females), the opportunity is taken to weigh and measure the body, to X-ray it for signs of metal such as lead shot, and perhaps to take blood samples in order to test for parasites and signs of disease.

Why do we need to study swans? Research is enjoyable for its own sake, but there are practical implications as well. Investigations into the Whistling swan of North America were initiated because of collisions with aircraft; understanding of the timing of migration and the routes traveled can help avoid such dangers. Increasing numbers of swans may mean more agricultural conflict, and ways to prevent this need investigation. Swans are particularly suited to long-term studies of their breeding success as they are long-lived and relatively site-faithful. The Whooper is, at the moment, the least studied of the swans of the northern hemisphere, and recent ringing programs in Britain, Iceland, Denmark, and Japan have provided valuable information on the use and conservation value of winter refuges and of staging places where the birds spend a few days in spring or autumn. More knowledge is needed of the breeding grounds, particularly in continental Europe and Asia. The Whooper swans of Iceland, where most summer work has been done so far, may well be a little different from the majority of the species — they appear to lay fewer eggs and be slightly smaller, and they have less yellow on their bills.

Swans in art.
Whooper swans have long been familiar to the peoples of Northern Europe and Asia. Thousands arrive to see swans that are fed and protected on reserves in Britain and in Japan; they are featured on television and in the press every winter. They appear in legends, poetry, art, and

music, and their voice has given rise to one of the oldest recorded myths: the "swan song," a concept that has come to mean the last masterpiece of an artist. For instance, *Schwanengesang* by Schubert was given that title by the publisher, as it was the composer's last song cycle, published posthumously in 1829.

In Christian iconography, angels fly on the wings of swans, and a saintly English bishop called Hugh of Lincoln was even adopted by a Whooper swan that arrived unexpectedly on September 29, 1186. In the absence of his own kind, the male swan attached itself to Hugh, guarding him as he might a mate and searching his sleeves for bread. The bird lived in the moat of the Episcopal manor of Stow and is said, during St. Hugh's last visit, to have shown his awareness of his master's imminent death by becoming unusually distraught. He remained at Stow for another seventeen years, which means that he was at least thirty-one years old when he died. Pictures and statues of St. Hugh always show the swan by his side.

Perhaps because of the swans' annual migration, high flight, and pure white plumage, man has often expressed a wish to change places with them and to imagine that they are human beings in disguise. In the myth of Leda and the swan, the bird is actually the god Zeus transformed. Gods and goddesses appear in the form of swans in many Irish legends where they are recognized to be supernatural by the chains of gold and silver worn around their necks. Some families of Europe, such as the de Cleves and the Brabants, claimed descent from the Swan Knight, the brother of a swan that also had a golden collar, and the tale was used to give a magical pedigree to Godfrey de Bouillon, the leader of the first Crusade and King of Jerusalem in 1100. A popular hero (called Helias, Elias Grail, Lohengrin, or Gerhard in various versions) arrives in a boat drawn by a chained swan, claims a bride won in battle, and warns her never to ask his name. Of course, she one day forgets, breaks the taboo, and a swan reappears to lead her sorrowing husband away.

The legend of the swan maiden seems to be Indo-European in origin but has many translations worldwide. In most of them a girl or spirit bride in swan form is captured by stealing her feathery cloak while she is bathing in a sacred spring. The man who hides her plumage can marry her, but she invariably finds it and leaves him desolate (like the "swan song," this tale may have its origins in the puzzle of migration and was intended to explain the absence of these conspicuously beautiful birds in summer). The most famous and enduring ballet in the repertoire, "Swan Lake," has a similarly sad theme with a white and a black swan who signify good and evil. Although good triumphs in the end, it is only after the death of the hero and of an enchanted girl who spends the day as a white swan.

Their association with water, which is so vital to fruitful life, meant that swans were sacred to many pagan peoples, including the Celts, and swans and water appear in a number of creation myths. An old Norse one tells of the creation of the world near a great ash tree that grew by a spring where a pair of swans floated; here, at the sanctuary of the gods, dwelt the Fates whose names are Past, Present, and Future.

The poet W. B. Yeats had an Irishman's fascination with swans; his most famous sonnet of 1923 is entitled "Leda and the Swan," and another, "The Wild Swans at Coole," is about Whoopers that returned every October to one of his favorite haunts, Coole Park in Galway. To Yeats, the birds seemed to have a sort of timelessness—they flew on forever as tireless travelers, and their springtime departures made him conscious of his own mortality rather than of theirs. Sir Herbert Hamilton-Harty, the Irish composer, wrote a tone poem for orchestra called "The Children of Lir" about four children changed into singing swans by their stepmother and condemned to wander the stormy coast of Antrim for a thousand years until the sound of a church bell releases them. The "Swan of Tuonela" is from a suite of four pieces by Jean Sibelius, based on the Finnish epic *Kalevala,* and originally written as a prelude to an opera. A long-necked, beautiful black Whooper swan floats on the river that divides the living and the dead; the graceful music has a dark melancholy quality, with a *cor anglais* taking the solo part.

I am lucky enough to live in a house overlooking a lake where a thousand wild Whooper and Bewick's swans spend the winter; I am therefore familiar with these lovely birds at close quarters. It is thrilling to hear the sounds of their arrival every autumn and to watch the flocks sweep down out of the northern sky. Tired families land on the water, take a drink, shake their plumage, and then settle to sleep for nearly twenty-four hours—they seem to recognize their home with the same confidence that I do. In different ways, we both benefit; they receive food and security for the next six months, and I obtain the greatest inspiration and pleasure. I hope that Teiji Saga's wonderful photographs will allow you to experience something of that same inspiration—without the glories of the natural world, man's existence is a sterile one indeed.

—Janet Kear

SWANS

1
In the winter, Whooper swans are extremely gregarious. These birds are somewhat
alarmed and hold their necks stiffly as they look at the source of the disturbance.
Odaitou, Hokkaido, March 4, 1983

2
Resting swans lose very little heat, and the snow does not melt against their insulating
feathers. Their bills are buried deep in their plumage.
Odaitou, Hokkaido, February 21, 1974

3
*In this large winter flock, the majority of swans appear to sleep, but most actually
have their eyes open, and one has raised its head.*
Odaitou, Hokkaido, February 21, 1974

4

Swans resting in the snow at the edge of water huddle very close together
for protection from the chill.
Odaitou, Hokkaido, March 8, 1981

5
Swans resting on the snow at sunrise. They have slept motionless through the night — any activity increases unwanted heat loss from their bodies.
Odaitou, Hokkaido, February 27, 1981

6

A swan's winter consists primarily of sleeping, preening, and feeding.
Odaitou, Hokkaido, March 5, 1985

7

The lack of footprints suggests that the swan walked to the spot where it is sitting
before the snow stopped falling. Since then, it has moved its wing tips slightly
and ruffled the snow.
Odaitou, Hokkaido, February 27, 1984

8
Open water is essential for drinking and for safety.
Odaitou, Hokkaido, February 23, 1974

9
The few gray birds are youngsters spending their first winter within the flock.
Odaitou, Hokkaido, February 22, 1974

10
The water is cold, but a single Whooper swan swims past the resting flock.
Odaitou, Hokkaido, March 30, 1985

11
March sunshine casts shadows on the snow.
Odaitou, Hokkaido, March 15, 1986

12
Necks do not all curve back in the same direction when swans tuck their bills beneath
their feathers. Note the strong, webbed feet.
Odaitou, Hokkaido, March 5, 1984

13
Swans and ducks gather to feed.
Inawashiro-ko, Fukushima, January 18, 1984

14
A January gathering of Bewick's swans, the smaller cousins of the Whooper;
the gray ones are young birds.
Chuzenji-numa, Fukushima, January 15, 1986

15
This internationally famous and much-admired photograph of Whoopers
has been called "Swan Shadow."
Kussharo-ko, Hokkaido, February 22, 1980

16
A flock of Whooper swans. Two young birds are on the left.
Kussharo-ko, Hokkaido, February 27, 1984

17
A flock at sunrise.
Inawashiro-ko, Fukushima, January 18, 1985

18
Winter sunrise.
Odaitou, Hokkaido, March 10, 1981

19
Flying and swimming swans and ducks.
Inawashiro-ko, Fukushima, January 17, 1982

20
Swans by moonlight.
Odaitou, Hokkaido, March 1, 1984

21
Swans feed among reed stalks that have remained standing throughout the winter.
Kushiro, Hokkaido, March 13, 1985

22

A flock of swans in early winter feed on waste grain left after harvest.
Near Inawashiro-ko, Fukushima, December 5, 1985

23
Bewick's swans gather beneath autumn trees.
Inawashiro-ko, Fukushima, November 5, 1984

24
Seven Bewick's swans display behind a family party of six larger Whoopers.
The two gray birds in the center are young Whoopers whose bills are now white
but will turn the same yellow shade as the adults' within five months.
Hyo-ko, Niigata, November 8, 1984

25
In autumn swans feed on cultivated land.
Near Hyo-ko, Niigata, November 10, 1985

26
Flocks of Whooper swans fly over the sea.
Furen-ko, Hokkaido, March 16, 1986

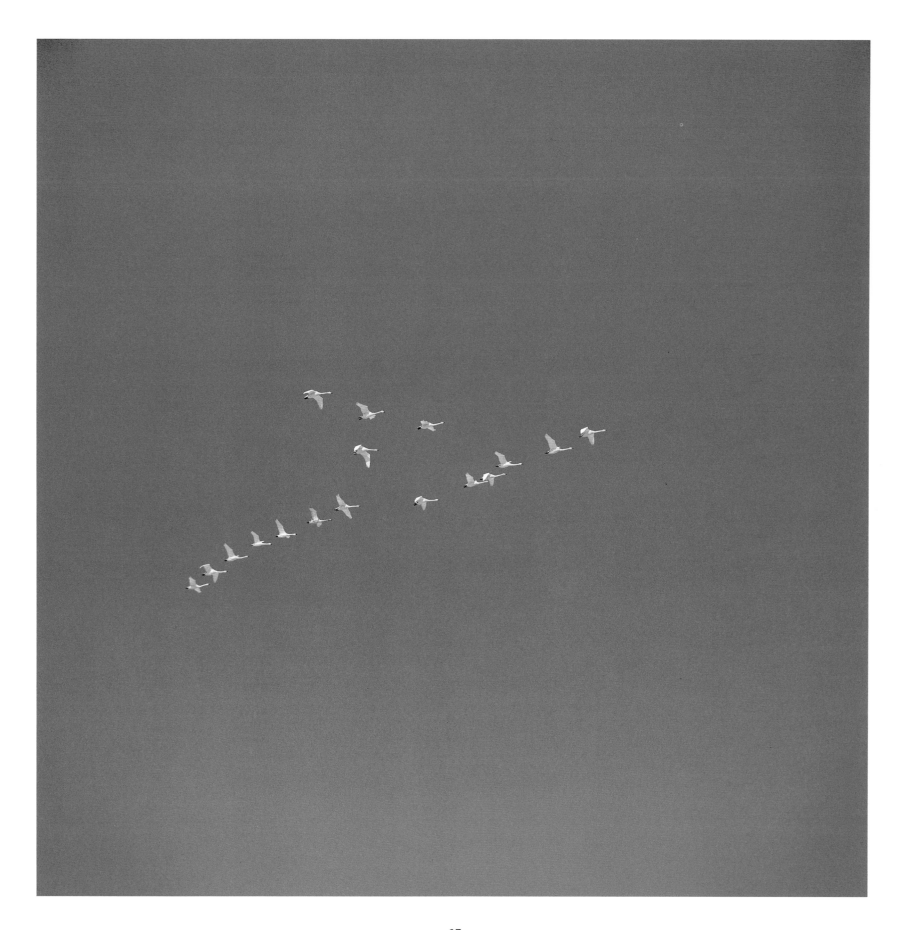

27

*A V-shape formation is adopted to reduce air turbulence at high altitudes. One young
Whooper flies among sixteen adults.
Kussharo-ko, Hokkaido, March 14, 1985*

28
Sensitive bill tips gently nibble and clean the plumage of the neck.
Odaitou, Hokkaido, February 18, 1980

29
*A resting Whooper swan breathes air warmed by its feathers and keeps its feet
tucked up to minimize heat loss.
Odaitou, Hokkaido, February 24, 1978*

30
Standing on one leg looks easy; the other foot is held out at the back "to dry." Note
the large webs and strong claws.
Odaitou, Hokkaido, February 15, 1978

31
Just above the base of the swan's tail is an oil gland which the bird first nibbles, then uses
to oil its feathers for better waterproofing.
Odaitou, Hokkaido, February 26, 1981

32

A swan settles its feathers with a wing-flap after preening. The broken pattern of its bill is most unusual.

Odaitou, Hokkaido, February 26, 1981

33
A breeze ruffles the plumage of a resting bird. Soon the swan will move to face
into the wind.
Odaitou, Hokkaido, March 1, 1981

34

A Whooper swan preens delicately beneath its wing. The rounded tail has
twenty main feathers.
Odaitou, Hokkaido, February 2, 1981

35
A flap shows the eleven primary quills of each wing.
Odaitou, Hokkaido, March 2, 1983

36
In order to drink, the swan takes a sip from the surface, then raises its head to allow water
to trickle down its throat.
Kussharo-ko, Hokkaido, March 18, 1983

37
The wings are powered by large breast muscles.
Odaitou, Hokkaido, March 8, 1980

38
*The profile of the head and bill of the Whooper is wedgeshaped. Its neck is long
and, here, most gracefully curved.*
Odaitou, Hokkaido, March 14, 1983

39

A Whooper swan's wing may span eight feet. Note the small fourth toe behind and above the foot.
Odaitou, Hokkaido, February 27, 1982

40
All the feathers of the head, neck, wings, and body are shaken by this stretching bird.
Odaitou, Hokkaido, March 1, 1983

41
Wing and leg on one side are frequently stretched together. Note the three-toed webbing
of the large black feet.
Odaitou, Hokkaido, February 21, 1982

42

In taking off, a swan runs along the ground while its wings beat the air for lift.
Odaitou, Hokkaido, February 18, 1982

43
*Mated male and female Whooper swans call together in display with wings spread in
defiance of others who may threaten their status.*
Odaitou, Hokkaido, March 8, 1981

44

Bathing is necessary to wet the feathers before preening. The upper bill is hinged with the
skull bones and can be raised separately.
Odate, Aktia, February 8, 1980

45
Two pairs of Whooper swans call and display together.
Kussharo-ko, Hokkaido, February 18, 1980

46
Feeding Whooper swans upend themselves to feed below the surface without breathing
for twenty seconds at a time.
Kussharo-ko, Hokkaido, February 19, 1978

47
Fights involve biting.
Kussharo-ko, Hokkaido, February 20, 1982

48
The bird on the left has lost the fight and turns away to leave the battle zone.
Kussharo-ko, Hokkaido, February 21, 1981

49
Running hard helps lift the swan from the ground into the air.
Odaitou, Hokkaido, March 2, 1981

50
A landing bird brings its legs and feet forward.
Odaitou, Hokkaido, March 8, 1984

51
Swan and shadow.
Odaitou, Hokkaido, February 15, 1980

52
Two swans resting but not asleep. Eyes are dark brown.
Odaitou, Hokkaido, February 21, 1982

53
Preening the side feathers in unison.
Odaitou, Hokkaido, March 2, 1984

54
Resting together with bill tip under the back's plumage.
Odaitou, Hokkaido, March 8, 1982

55
A pair of Whooper swans fly together over the water.
Odaitou, Hokkaido, February 24, 1981

56
Feet and legs placed back against the tail streamline a body for flight.
Odaitou, Hokkaido, March 9, 1982

57
Three swans ready to land.
Kussharo-ko, Hokkaido, March 18, 1983

58
Juvenile and adult Whooper swans spread the webs of their feet to act as
windbreaks while landing.
Odaitou, Hokkaido, February 13, 1982

59

The plastic neck collar on the nearest bird has been put on as part of a research program
investigating the movements of individual swans.
Odaitou, Hokkaido, February 22, 1974

60
Stiff-necked, these swans watch the photographer.
Odaitou, Hokkaido, February 28, 1983

61
Whooper swans gather to be fed on the water.
Kussharo-ko, Hokkaido, February 15, 1982

62
*Courting between a young male and female in early spring. They are calling softly, head
and bills held low and submissive.
Odaitou, Hokkaido, March 2, 1982*

63

*A mated pair display in triumph, calling with open mouths and raised tongues. The bird
on the left has a similar bill pattern to that in plate 32 and may be the same bird.
Odaitou, Hokkaido, February 10, 1981*

64
Lowering and raising head and neck alternately, the pair call together.
Kussharo-ko, Hokkaido, March 6, 1983

65
Fights involve biting and thrashing wings.
Odaitou, Hokkaido, March 2, 1984

66
A standoff fight about to be joined.
Odaitou, Hokkaido, March 1, 1983

67
Two, probably male, Whooper swans in imminent combat.
Odaitou, Hokkaido, February 15, 1980

68
A mated pair lands on the water.
Odaitou, Hokkaido, March 8, 1981

69
Two Whooper swans on the wing.
Odaitou, Hokkaido, February 8, 1980

70

In copulation, the male holds the female's neck feathers with the tip of his bill.
Kussharo-ko, Hokkaido, April 10, 1987

71

Copulation always occurs while the birds are swimming. The male's outspread
wings help him keep his balance.
Kussharo-ko, Hokkaido, April 10, 1974

72
A pair requires a large summer territory in which to rear their young.
Harads, Sweden, June 18, 1981

73

Male and female noisily demonstrate their possession of a breeding territory
with wing-waving displays and calling.
Harads, Sweden, May 14, 1981

74
The Whooper swan's nest of five eggs is not far from the water in a typical
taigu forest of aspen and pine.
Harads, Sweden, May 17, 1981

75
Female Whoopers incubate eggs for about thirty days.
Harads, Sweden, June 25, 1981

76
Newly-hatched cygnets are not dry yet. At this stage they are unafraid of humans.
Harads, Sweden, June 25, 1981

77
A mother warms her cygnets in a nest beneath a lichen-covered fir tree.
Harads, Sweden, June 25, 1981

78
One fluffy cygnet has climbed onto its mother's back for a better look
at its summer world.
Harads, Sweden, June 25, 1981

79
By September, the cygnets will be fully grown and ready to fly south.
Harads, Sweden, June 25, 1981